Dedication

This Handbook is respectfully dedicated
To all Church Musicians, or even those
Who want to be Church Musicians,
Or those who should be Church Musicians,
Regardless of age, creed, or political leanings

This should cover all those left out of our first
Handbook, which was primarily for Choir Directors,
Ministers of Music, or Chorus Directors

May this great treatise be of further inspiration
Even beyond *The Choir Director's Handbook?*
We have tried to poke fun at everyone! If you have
Been left out, or feel neglected, give us time, or
Let us know! We will get to you eventually

CONCLUSION

We have discovered the one thing that describes *all* readers, regardless of musical ability. *Everyone* turns beyond the first few pages, and generally to the back of the book to see how it comes out. So, for the convenience of all, we have started this book with the ending. The beginning or Foreward is at the end, since that is where most everyone will begin, and makes for a great time-saving device. Since all musicians should be familiar with time, this will be of some importance.

Other concluding remarks may be found in various chapters and will add to your excitement in reading this book. Should you like to add your own remarks, please feel free to do so. We have left space on many of the pages for you to make these remarks.

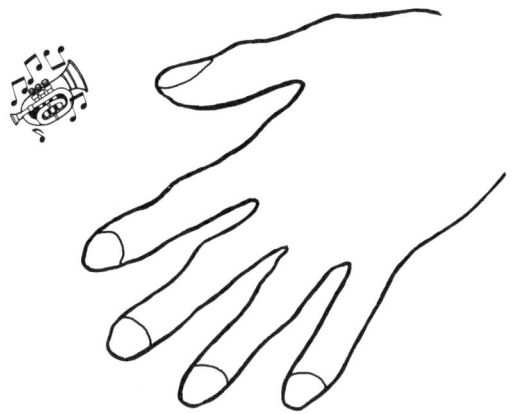

The Handbook for the Ultimate Church Musician

By CHARLES MONTGOMERY

© Copyright 1985 by LIGHT HEADED MUSIC PUBLISHING COMPANY
A Division of Light Hearted Music Publishing Company
P. O. Box 150246 - - Nashville, Tennessee 37215
Telephone 615 - 776-5678

ALWAYS READ THE FINE PRINT

Again, we want to let our readers know about our use, or mis-use of our great hymns and songs in a frivolous way. We think that a sense of humor is vital to living in our busy world today. So, everything we have done here is to make fun of ourselves and our friends. It is hard to sing and make music without smiling, so we hope you enjoy our book as much as we did writing it. Sometimes if you don't laugh, you have to cry. It is better to laugh.

Charles Montgomery

THE TABLE OF CONTENTS

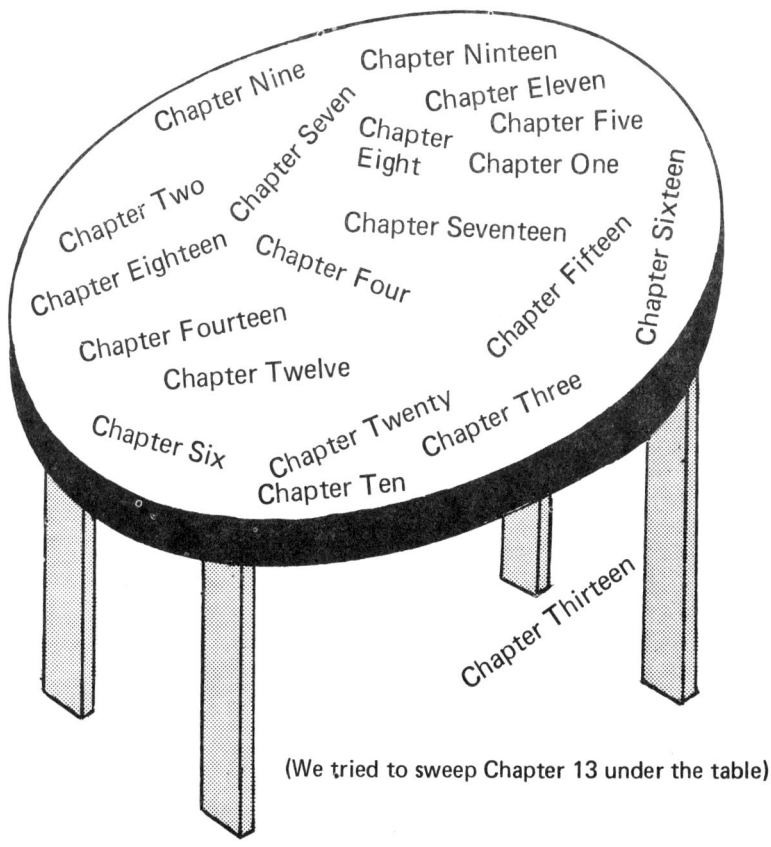

(We tried to sweep Chapter 13 under the table)

(The Table of Contents is round, because we didn't want to be cornered on any subject.)

BACKWARD

In order to be consistent, we have no *Foreward* in this book, and since the beginning was the end, we have a backward.

And since there was no foreward, it is hard to look back on it, so, we will just move ahead and try to give some sort of explanation as to why this book was written.

After the release of THE CHOIR DIRECTOR'S HANDBOOK?, there were many inquiries concerning musicians other than choir directors. Actually, there were really not all that many, but I am sure inquiries will come, and I want to be ready for them.

So, with very little thought, we have prepared this handbook for general church musicians and we hope you will be inspired to seek further help after reading this book.

STUDY OUTLINE

It is strongly suggested that you take notes while reading this book. In order for you to do this more easily, we have notes scattered throughout the book and you may take as many of these notes as you like. Should these not be enough for you, send a self-addressed, stamped envelope to the publisher and we will send additional notes to you.

In addition, we have several areas broken down into different categories. This may lead you to think this is a broken-down book, but such is not the case. We have different sections, such as dealing with youth, senior adults, and children, which will require specialized study. So please adapt yourself to any and all sections. There will be special attention given for writing music in age groupings.

Two center pages are blank and this was done because we want to keep control. The center is a natural opening and we do not want anyone to read material out of order.

We have checked with several physicians as to how this book may be studied in terms of health, and all were unanimous in prescribing that it be taken with one grain of sodium chloride. We concur in this.

These are for taking notes. (It is suggested they be kept in a note-book)

CHAPTER ONE

REVIEW

Since very little material has been presented up to this chapter, we thought this might be a good time to have a review. It should be easy for the reader, and will be an example as to the type of consideration we have in the presentation of this material.

After reviewing the material presented up to this point, you should be ready to plunge right into the more difficult sections of this book.

(You will notice this is a page where we have included notes for you to take.)

These are available if you only need to take a few quick notes.

CHAPTER TWO

CHILDREN'S MUSIC

In this chapter, we will try to clarify some false ideas involving children's music. Since most people start out as children, and during childhood, have their first experience with music, this seems a logical selection to have early on in this book.

Now, as to correcting some of the false premises involving children's music, the main thing is this: **Most Children's Music is generally made up of large notes.** This is the reason so many children have problems with music. The notes should be much smaller for them. The large notes are the reason many children are unable to carry a tune. As they grow older, the notes can be made larger and they can easily handle them. If the notes are too large and heavy, how can they expect to even *carry* a tune and get up to their scales? You can easily see the following example is more appropriate to children's sizes.

(Please do not take any of these notes. They are for children!)

CHAPTER THREE

OLDER ADULT MUSIC

This is an area that I could hardly wait for, since I know that some day I will be an older adult. I have heard for many years, "They don't write songs like they used to;" "I wish they would sing more of the old songs;" "When I was your age we sang.........;" "We used to sing songs that had a *real* tune;" and last, but not least, "I had to walk 28 miles in the snow to catch the bus to get to choir practice." (And this was in July and that church didn't even have a choir!)

However, some of this stuff these people like has been around for a few years, and still gets sung.

Most of the music for older adults needs to have a few things to identify it. First, it needs to be old. For the most part, the older the better. If the pages or sheets are tattered and torn, great! Better still, if it smells musty, you have a real treasure.

And, it must be dated. The Forties! The Twenties! The Nineties! And believe you me, that is all. Those three eras. There was nothing worthwhile written in any other era. The Thirties had to be a period of Depression. (I am sure this is when they wrote the Blues.) You never hear of music being written in the teens. And can't you just hear, "I love the music that was written in Nineteen Ought Six? Just not so. It has to be from the Forties, Twenties, and the Nineties! We have a song here that is somewhat akin to these eras. It will probably go in one era and out the other. In writing music for Older Adults, keep in mind the one thing that is required. Write old music!

(Sorry, we were unable to find any old notes to put here.)

OLD SONG

Lyrics by DAISEY GONEBY
Music arr. by OL D. TUNE

"I know I said you needed a little 'swing' in your music, Bro. Rudy, but.........."

CHAPTER FOUR

PITCH

In this chapter, we will deal with pitch. For those who insist on a Biblical background, this dates back to Noah, who covered the Ark with pitch. And, in all probability, this was relative pitch, because his sons pitched in to help. And, no doubt, because there was an early interest in music, the two fish that were in the small aquarium on board the Ark, just had to be *Tuner Fish.*

Thus, pitch is important.

In addition to relative pitch, we have perfect pitch. I can assure you, however, that *none* of your relatives will have perfect pitch. Actually, there is some doubt as to anyone having perfect pitch, since there is nothing perfectly tuned for the person with perfect pitch to be compared with. So, this brings us back to everything being relative, which is to say, nobodys' relatives are perfect.

Last, but not least, we have concert pitch. There has been a concerted effort to do away with concert pitch. Due to the fact that concert pitch is higher than the pitch that is usually used, in order to cut expenses, most people do not use it. You may hear it in the higher income brackets.

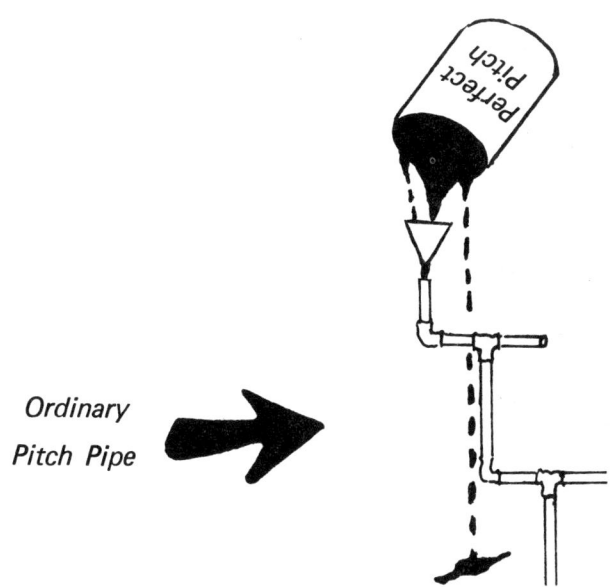

Ordinary Pitch Pipe

"I know I said the tenors should get higher, Bro. Rudy, but......."

CHAPTER FIVE

SINCERITY

This happens to be an area of extreme importance. All church musicians should try to be sincere. The following would be the best advise I could give you in this book:
"Be sincere, even if you don't mean it!"

Put your comments here: ___

CHAPTER SIX

YOUNGER ADULT MUSIC

This is an area where we do not have any music suggestions. This is an age group that is completely bewildering. They have suddenly found they do not have the time to learn all the repeats of the youth music, and they have also discovered some of the old stuff is really not all that bad.

And too, the older adults have discovered that these people are really some great kind of folks, so there is a period of mass confusion. Actually, they do things, including music, quite well.

Come to think of it, this age group does not need all that much help, so we will only suggest you pick the best of the other chapters for Younger Adults.

Put your comments here: ___

CHAPTER SEVEN

PROPER ATTIRE FOR THE ULTIMATE CHURCH MUSICIAN

There is no doubt that this is an important area, so we may spend some time here. First of all, each musician should be appropriately attired. Now, the key word here, is not the key of "G" but what is *appropriate.* On second thought, this may be a shorter chapter than originally planned.

We will say, however, that consideration for your audience must be given. If you do not think your folks are ready for sequins, we suggest you bring this on gradually. For the choir members, they can be worn on the back, and will hardly be noticed, but will give the choir a feeling that everyone is halfway with it. This does create a slight problem with the director, but since the sequins will be on a jacket of some sort, the jacket can be taken off and casually draped over the pulpit and over a period of a few weeks or years, (depending on the congregation) more or less sequins may be displayed. We will not make a definite commitment to cowboy boots, but they may or may not be worn. We would suggest caution as to stuffing the pants leg in the boots. And, we would suggest black boots for the morning services. Evening services might be a little more casual. Never, Never wear spurs. They are never in tune with the organ.

(It is not known if Spurgeon wore spurs or not.)

"I know I said the choir should look more contemporary, Bro. Rudy, but............"

CHAPTER EIGHT

SPECIAL SONG SELECTIONS FOR ALL OCCASIONS

During Hard-of-Hearing-Week
    O Come, Loud Anthems Let Us Sing

If you have a magician preaching
    Immortal, Invisible

Pastor's sermon: "Father's Day Gifts"
    Blest Be the Tie that Binds

The Preacher preaching on paying off your car note
    When I Can Read My Title Clear

If the Preacher preaches on farming
    We Plow the Fields

During Rodeo Week
    Ride On! Ride On In Majesty

During Credit Union Week
    A Charge to Keep I Have

A Song for Salesmen
    Somebody's Knocking at Your Door

During the Darkness of a Power Shortage
    Send the Light

(The following page shows how well loved some songs are)

MORE SPECIAL MUSIC

SHAPED NOTES

Another special thing in music, is shaped notes. These are not used as much as they once were. However, they still have their uses. I will give their names, but not their shapes. Since they are not used very much now, these notes are out of shape. Their more colloquial names are:

Dough, Ray, Me, Far, Soul, Lah, Tea, Dough. These can be arranged into chords, such as Dough, Soul, Me, Dough!

An Italian Butcher made one chord quite famous with shaped notes. He always sang this certain chord as he made an Italian sausage. The chord was Sol-La-Mi. I will show this chord as it was originally sung in shaped notes.

Mi ◇

La ■

Sol ●

Put your comments here: ___

MUSIC FOR AN OCEAN VOYAGE

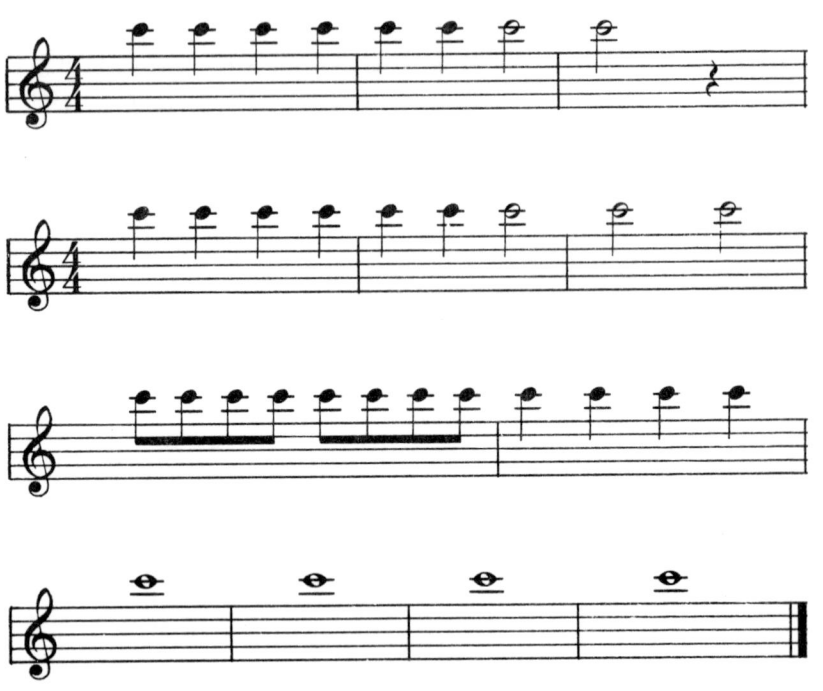

(All notes are on the High C's)

CHAPTER NINE

SMILING

Next to sincerity, I would say the smile would be as important as anything in the Ultimate Church Musician's repertoire.

The smile is crucial. Whatever the song, smile. If you have been standing up for forty-five minutes, waiting to sing while someone makes an announcement, smile. It will keep the congregation confused, and will cover your forgetting the song.

Smile while singing. That is true, even when singing the "O" vowel. I'll admit, it isn't easy. Also, smile when singing consonants, like "m's" and "n's" (You remember them, they melt in your mouth. Or did you think we were talking about Africa? You know, the dark consonant!)

But keep smiling!

o o

You will notice or you should have noticed that these two center-fold pages have very little on them. This was done in order to control the study procedure for this book. Many people will automatically turn to the center of the book (this is a natural thing, because the book just opens that way) and they will do things out of order. This was done to prevent this.

You will notice or you should have noticed that these two center-fold pages have very little on them. This was done in order to control the study procedure for this book. Many people will automatically turn to the center of the book (this is a natural thing, because the book just opens that way) and they will do things out of order. This was done to prevent this.

CHAPTER TEN

MUSIC EXERCISES

In this day of stress and strain, everyone needs plenty of excercise. This includes good musical exercise. This can be done in many ways, and there are many forms of musical exercise. We have listed some of these below:

Working on your scales. Most scales can be adjusted where they will weigh less than they show. Or is that they will show less than they weigh. Oh, well.

For vocal control, try holding a note for a long time. We had a banker in our choir that held a note for ninety days.

Sing pear shaped tones. It is awkward, singing with a pear in your mouth, but it is very good exercise.

This should be enough to get you started. If you have others to suggest, send them in, along with a label. Just pick whatever label that is convenient.

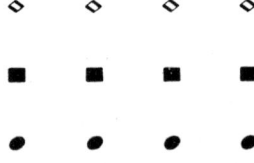

CHAPTER ELEVEN

IMPORTANT MUSIC SYMBOLS

Probably the most important of all music symbols is the Cleff. Cleffs originated in England in a little town named Dover. Originally, they were white. Below, we have a painting of them.

The White Cleffs of Dover

Another important symbol in music, is the dot. They are used in all types of music, but are used extensively in Polka music. These dots are called Polka Dots.

I suppose the next most important symbol in music, would be the bar. Carrie Nations tried to do away with all of them, but they still have an important part in music.

(You should take a few notes)

27

"I know I said give the soloist a hand, Mrs. Dimwittie, but......."

CHAPTER TWELVE

MUSIC FOR YOUTH

We really tried to avoid this chapter, because this is an area where we hesitate to intrude. However, I guess we should just blindly jump in.

Most of the youth of today are really in Rock Music. This is actually not really new, but is just music with a BOULDER approach. The BEAT is the thing here, and if you try to keep up with them, you will easily become a part of the "beat" generation. It is *quite* strenuous. One needs to be in great shape to participate in Youth Music, and we strongly recommend the use of *Shape* notes for this music.

Another thing that is good here, is a great memory. Not only is the same phrase used over and over again, but you need to remember just how many times to repeat it. This is one reason why older adults have failed to catch on to the theme of rock music. They just can't seem to remember it, and when your memory goes, you may as well forget it.

It is good that rock has come in recent years, because without electricity to amplify it, it would have been useless. Beethoven and Bach would have been handicapped, because neither had electricity. Come to think of it, I believe one was deaf, and had he come along in recent years, he probably could have heard the youth music of today. It does tend to be a little **LOUD** at times.

The sample we have here for youth music, is self-explanatory, and almost anyone can write for youth. Actually, some of it is not really all that bad, and bears a striking resemblance to music we listened to a few or many years ago. There is an old Indian saying, "Any good music that is done well, will be done again."

Put your comments here: ___

(Some symbols useful in writing Youth Music)

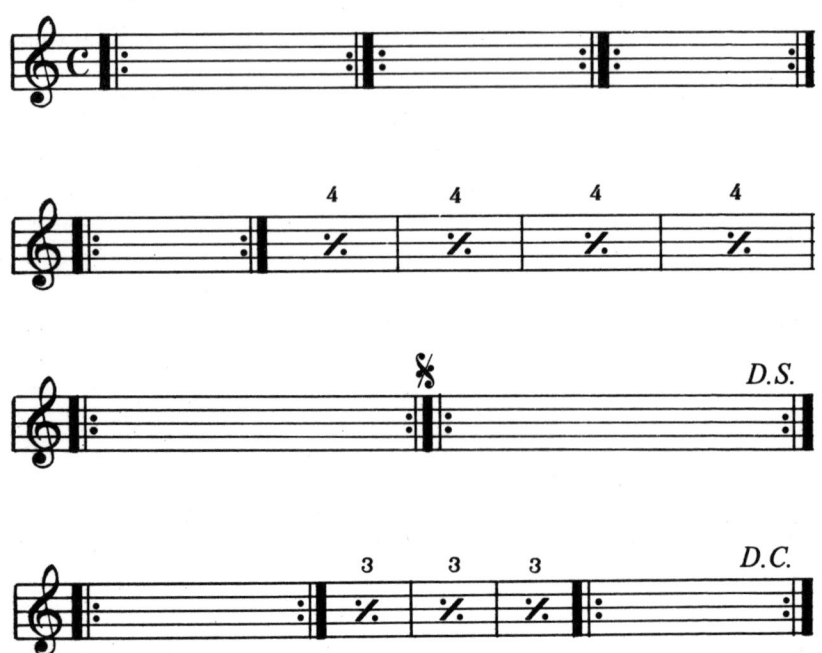

(This exercise may be repeated if necessary)

Sing It Again

Lyrics by R. E. PEAT
Music by A. GINN and A. GINN

The main symbol for "Youth Music"
The Electric Chord!

THE STANDING OVATION

This is something that has become quite common in recent years. Actually, it can be somewhat confusing, since many times the congregation or audience thinks the program or performance is over, and have stood up, trying to leave. There may have only been a dramatic pause in the music, a fuse blown on an amplifier, or a musician dropping from sheer exhaustion. The performers think this is a standing ovation, and keep going, and the audience, becoming embarrassed, starts applauding, hoping this will bring things to an end, and actually it becomes a stand-off.

It is something that has to be dealt with, and almost any action will be wrong. On the following page, we have some discussion as to where the term originated.

THE

STANDING OVATION

(The Ovation Guitar has a back that is rounded, so, naturally, it is unable to lie down, so it has to be a "Standing Ovation!")

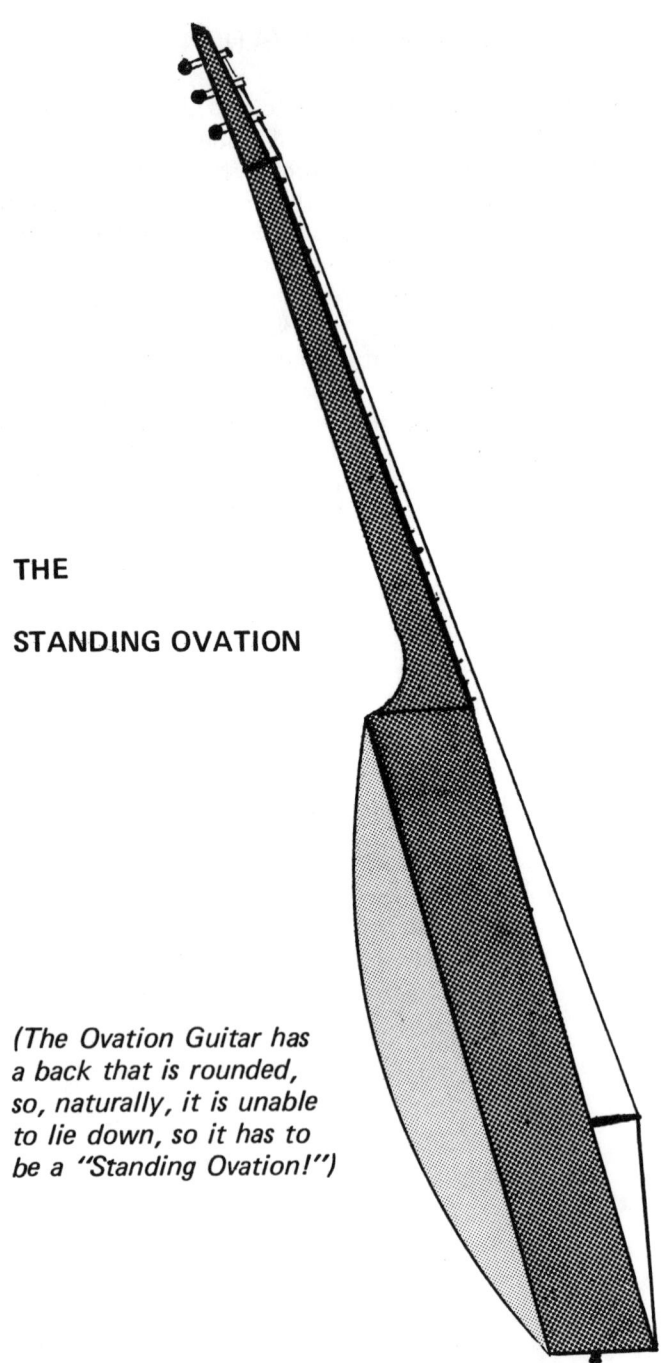

CHAPTER THIRTEEN

(Being superstitious, I refused to write this chapter. I really did not even want to put the Chapter Number in, but to avoid confusion, I did put the Chapter Number here. It is to be used only as a guide in finding the preceding and following chapters. They are Chapters Twelve and Fourteen, in somewhat that order.)

Put your comments here: ___

CHAPTER FOURTEEN

THE KEYBOARD SPECIALIST

This is one of my favorite areas of music specialists. They are actually the most important musicians. They control all of the keys. Anytime anyone wants to know the key for a song, whether it is the Director, Choir Member, Chorus Member, Soloist, or who, they must get the key from the Keyboard Specialist.

Now, as the title suggests, the keys are kept on a board. It can be large or small, depending on the background and training of the keyboard specialist. The keyboard should also be close at hand. The keys can be hung on nails on the board, or if the church can afford it, brass screws may be used which will be more attractive. It is suggested that the keys be painted in different colors for more ease in recognizing them. Use your own feelings as to what these colors are.

It is also suggested that a portion of the board be used or designated for the pastor only. This section will be for the following keys: Keys to the kitchen, keys to the janitorial supplies, spare car keys, and others. These will not need to be color-coded, since their use will be so often, they will be remembered.

The title "Keyboard Specialist" can also be spelled "Key *Bored* Specialist" since there may be times the job is not too exciting. If the specialist decides to write any music, and there are any family skeletons in the closet, just use a skeleton key for the song.

(These are the notes the Keyboard Specialist prefers)

CHAPTER FIFTEEN

JUST PLAIN ALL AROUND MUSIC

One of the types of music that is needed everywhere, is just good all around music. Often this can be found in Circle Theaters. Then again, it is hard to find. Sometimes you can just go around in circles, looking for it.

Generally, if a college offers this music in a course, they will advertise their classes in circulars. It is good for your circulation.

We have tried to show a little of this music on the following page, with further explanations.

Put your comments here: ___

♩ ♩ ♩

(These are notes used in "Swing" Music, because they look like little swings! They really do, don't they?)

The following is a sample of music which can be used for "Rounds" and is the type of music generally used in the better circles. Squares will absolutely refuse to do any music of this type.

It has been performed in the Oval Room of the White House at many of the sewing circles of the First Ladies in days gone by. Actually, it was developed by King Arthur and his Knights as they sat around the Round Table, and rounded out many of their meals in this fashion.

In the Westward Movement of our country, and the expansion of the railroads, it was performed in the Roundhouses of the railroad stations as the ticket agents sold Roundtrip tickets all over the West. The cowboys used this type of music on Roundups, eating Round steak as they sang to the cattle.

It is now used in Amusement Parks on merry-go-Rounds.

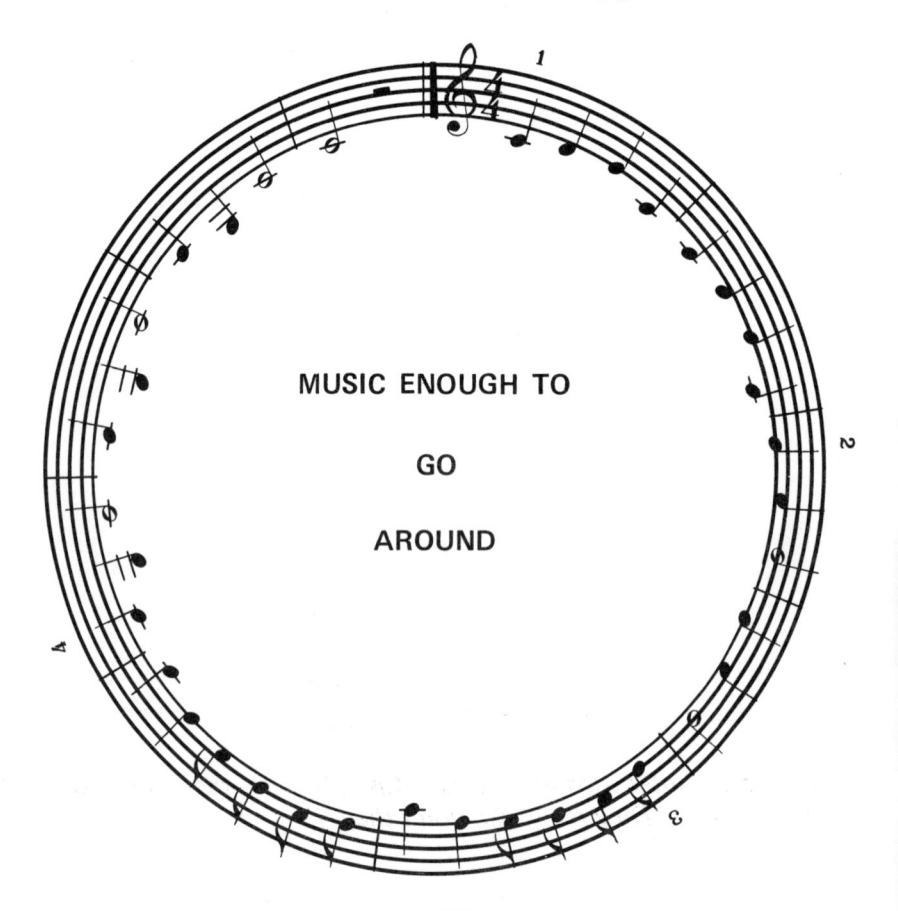

MUSIC ENOUGH TO

GO

AROUND

CHAPTER SIXTEEN

BALANCE, SCALES, AND SPECIAL PROBLEMS

The Ultimate Musician in the Church needs to pay special attention to scales. They are useful for singing exercises, and help to keep the music program balanced.

Now, moving to other problem areas, such as delays due to electronic malfuncions. This often happens, due to microphones, untrained sound systems and the prepared musician can handle these problems. Those who are inexperienced are welcome to use the following suggestions on how to handle these delays.

Do chalk-talk while situation is being remedied.

Bring a thermos of coffee or a sandwich and act as though this happens all the time, which is usually true.

If you have a portable typewriter, this is generally a good time to write letters.

Knit something.

Read a few chapters from the pulpit Bible. (Not to the congregation, but just to catch up on your own reading).

Anything to keep looking busy while you are up there.

Write to us and share your own ideas as to how to handle this.

♩ ♩ ♩ ♩ ♩ ♩ ♩ ♩ ♩ ♩
𝅗𝅥 𝅗𝅥 𝅗𝅥 𝅗𝅥 𝅗𝅥 𝅗𝅥 𝅗𝅥 𝅗𝅥 𝅗𝅥 𝅗𝅥

(These are 'grace' notes. You didn't deserve them, but we put them here, never-the-less!)

"Don't you think the basses were a little heavy on that last song?"

CHAPTER SEVENTEEN

ATTENDANCE PROBLEMS

This is an area that we shall deal with, because it involves all churches and all musicians. Naturally if they are there, or present, it does not involve them, so, we shall only deal with those absent. Personally, I like the practice of only one chair on stage or in the choir loft for each musician. If you have more chairs than are needed, you will have a lot of milling around, as the group tries to decide which chair will be left vacant. This matters not if there are one hundred empty chairs, or one. You have a problem as to whether each musician carries a chair with him, or whether you appoint a chairman or chairperson to carry all the chairs in. If the choir or orchestra is large, this will require an unusually strong chairman.

Back to attendance. If the whole choir is absent, it can be very noticeable. If this can be made evident to all church musicians, it should be of benefit. The following page shows how things look from out front.

"The Bass Section does seem to be a bit short, this morning, Bro. Rudy!"

CHAPTER EIGHTEEN

SUNDAY EVENING MUSIC

There is no question that attendance for Sunday Evening Services is not as good as Sunday Morning, and the main reason for this is Evening Services are held at night.

There is not much that can be done about this, but the music should be special. The following page is a sample of Evening Music, and is good even though the lighting is poor.

We have left a lot of space on this page for you to jot down your own ideas as to how to improve the evening service. Select your best ideas and mail them in to us and we will be glad to evaluate them.

(If you only want to make a short note, this should do.)

♩

SPECIAL MUSIC FOR EVENING SERVICES

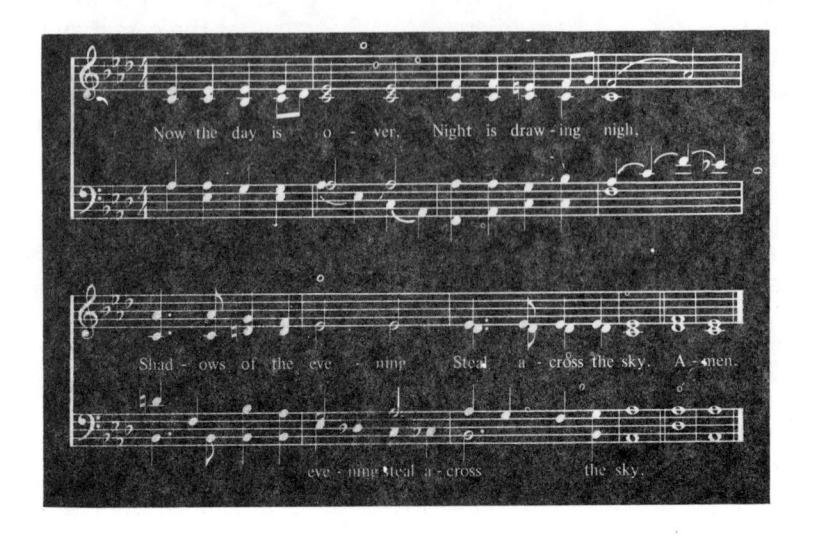

CHAPTER NINETEEN

LIBERAL AND CONSERVATIVE MUSIC

Naturally, you have different types of people in the average church. Some are more liberal or conservative as the case may be, and music must be available for all. Most of the music for the conservative congregation should be sung exactly as written and to not take liberties with the notes, or words. Sing each song exactly as written. Being somewhat conservative, myself, I think everyone should sing exactly what the author wrote. If you want to sing something else, write your own song. However, I do feel that I, personally, know enough about music, and words, that if I can improve it, I should do so.

Most of the Conservative Music was written in Music Conservatories. Liberal Music generally has a lot more words and music to the songs, as Liberal writers are generally quite liberal in using a lot of notes and music. Conservative songs are short, for the most part. This is to conserve paper.

If you are not sure which category you fit in, just write a couple of songs and send them to us and we will put you in your place. You may not be happy with it, but in order for us to write books on music and musicians, we have to know how you fit in. Actually, you may fit in somewhere in the middle, and this creates problems for us. We have to spread our music out a lot for all ages and this is called the middle-age-spread. Oh, well.....

Do notice the following page and this may help you to choose where you fit in and you will not have to write to us. We will miss your letter, however.

Music for Squares

Music for the Left
Jesus Is All the World to Me

Music for the Right
Jesus Is All the World to Me

GLOSSARY

Accent	A nice way of saying Act One or Two stinks
Allegretto	A ghetto, but one in an alley
Al Segno	A very expensive Cuban cigar
A poco a poco	A small Mexican resort village
A punta diarco	A football kick that is very high
Aria Buffa	An informal dinner after a performance
Ballet	A Sleeping mat
Bari-basso	A fish that is part Bass and part Baricuda
Bartok	Conversation in a saloon
Castanets	A term used in fishing. Cast a nets over here
Cello	A light dessert, like strawberry cello
Diatonic	A tonic taken when on a diet
Diminished Chords	Cords that have broken and are shorter
Expressivo	A very fancy coffee
Full Orchestra	Right after the band has eaten
Glockenspiel	A long vocal dissertation about Glocken
Homophony	A telephone used only at home
In disparte	Bringing a party to a close
Kettledrum	A drum used in a cowboy band
Lost Chord	A rope that's been missing for years
Madrigals	A female chorus from Madri
Marimba	A movie actress named Carmen
Mendelssohns	The male offspring of Mendel
Note value	How much notes cost
Overtone	A note played again and again
Piano forte	A dress little girls wear
Pizzicato	Pizza with apricots
Quaver	A bag to carry arrows in
Relative Major	One of your kinfolks who is an officer
Relative Minor	A kinsman who digs coal
Sonata	A male vocalist whose first name is Frank
Space notes	Notes used by astronauts
Triplet	A very short journey
Upright Piano	A piano with unquestioned moral background
Velocemente	A mint that dissolves very quickly
Wood Winds	Breezes in the forest
Xylophone	An unlisted short phone
Zither	Opposite of brother

CHAPTER TWENTY

CREDITS

I am sorry to announce there are no credits, because we were not able to get any help from anyone on this book, and no one would assume any responsibility for it.

FOREWORD

We are looking *foreward* to our next effort.